A New Sun

Un Nuevo Sol

Written by Max Benavidez & Katherine Del Monte
Illustrated by José Ramírez

Escrito por Max Benavidez & Katherine Del Monte
Ilustrado por José Ramírez

Lectura Books
Los Angeles

I came here with a dream,

Yo vine con un sueño,

with
so
many
hopes.

con
tantas
esperanzas.

I was
looking
for a
new
life.

Buscaba
una
nueva
vida.

I left
at night,
the sky
was filled
with
stars.

Cuando
salía
de noche,
el cielo
estaba lleno
de
estrellas.

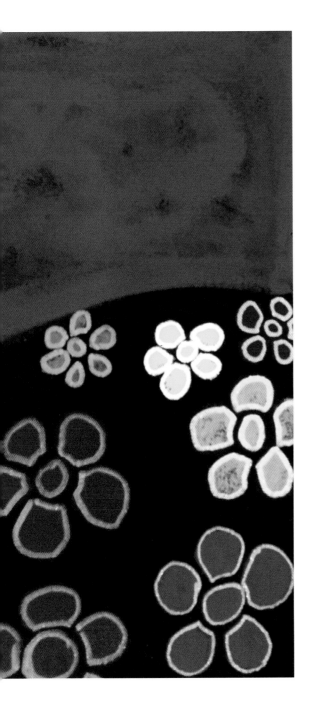

The moon was rising.

La luna estaba saliendo.

I arrived
with the
morning
sun.

Llegué
con
el sol
de la
mañana.

There,
I
walked
everywhere.

Caminaba
a todas
partes.

Here,
I
ride the
big
blue
bus.

Aquí,
viajo en
el gran
autobús
azul.

In my
village,
I knew
my
neighbors.

En mi
pueblo
conocía
a
mis
vecinos.

18

Here,
I meet **new**
people every day.
Big people,
small
people.

Aquí,
estoy
conociendo
a gente
nueva
cada día.
Adultos
y
niños.

People
from the
other
side of the
world,
speaking
languages
I never
heard.

Gentes
de diferentes
partes del
mundo,
hablando
idiomas
que nunca
había
escuchado.

I say
hola,
they
say
hello.

Cuando
Yo
digo
hola,
ellos
responden
hello.

They *eat* my food.

Ellos *comen* mi comida.

I eat their food, too.

Yo como su comida también.

I feel like
I live under a
new sun
in a new
world.

Siento
que vivo
bajo un
nuevo sol
en un
nuevo
mundo.

Yet,
no matter
how
different
we
are

Sin
embargo,
no importa
cuán
diferentes
somos

we
have
the
same
hopes.

tenemos
la
misma
esperanza.

We share the same **dream** of a better tomorrow.

Compartimos el mismo sueño **de** un mejor **futuro.**

New Vocabulary / Nuevo Vocabulario

English	Spanish
Dream	Sueño
Life	Vida
Night	La noche
Stars	Estrellas
Moon	La luna
Sun	El sol
Village	Pueblo
Bus	El autobús
Neighbors	Vecinos

People		Gente
World		El mundo
Hello		Hola
Eat		Comer
Food		Comida
Feel		Siento
Different		Diferente
Hope		Esperanza
Share		Compartir

A New Sun

Reflections of an immigrant arriving in a new land.

The text is in both English and Spanish, making this book useful for second-language learners of English and Spanish. A language curriculum is available by calling Lectura at (866) 480-8736. Ask about other books and curricula for second-language learners of Spanish and English.

Katherine Del Monte is the founder and director of The Latino Family Literacy Project, a program that emerged out of her experiences working with Latino families.

Max Benavidez is a writer. His essays and poetry have appeared in many literary journals and anthologies. He teaches courses on Latino culture and art at UCLA.

José Ramírez is an artist, educator, and a father who was born and lives in Los Angeles. He dedicates the paintings in this book to his parents, José and María.

Un Nuevo Sol

Reflexiones de un inmigrante sobre su llegada a un nuevo país.

Con un texto en dos idiomas, en español y en inglés, este libro les será útil a aquellos estudiantes que estén aprendiendo inglés o español como segundo idioma. Usted puede obtener mayor información acerca del plan de estudio de idiomas llamando Lectura, marcando sin costo al número telefónico (866) 480-8736. Al llamar, solicite informes acerca de otros libros y planes de estudio para aprender español y/o inglés.

Katherine Del Monte es la fundadora y directora del The Latino Family Literacy Project, un programa que surgió como resultado de su experiencia al trabajar con familias latinas.

Max Benavidez es escritor. Sus ensayos y su poesía han sido publicadas en diferentes revistas literarias y antologías. Es profesor de UCLA donde da clases de cultura latina y arte.

José Ramírez es artista, pedagogo y padre de familia. Nació y vive en Los Ángeles. El le ha dedicado la ilustración de este libro a sus padres, José y María.